THIS BOOK BELONGS TO

_____

_____

_____

📞 _____

✉ _____

📷 _____

dbp   DESIGNER BOOKS PUBLICATION

Date: _____

Date: _____

Date: _____

Date: _____

Date: _____

Date: _____

Date: _____

Date: _____

Date: _____

Date: _____

Made in the USA
Monee, IL
29 September 2021